Doors Out of
the Underworld

Scott Withiam

MadHat Press
Asheville, North Carolina

MadHat Press
MadHat Incorporated
PO Box 8364, Asheville, NC 28814

The Library of Congress has assigned
this edition a Control Number of
2019936246

ISBN 978-1-941196-88-5 (paperback)

Cover art: *Cypresses* by Vincent Van Gogh (1898)
Cover design by Marc Vincenz
Book design by MadHat Press

www.MadHat-Press.com

First Printing

To the real doors: eyes, hearts, voices, hands & minds; children, mine & yours, domestic animals & wildlife, landscapes familiar & foreign, architecture, music & art, dear parents, friends, neighbors, relatives, acquaintances, strangers, newcomers, teachers all. To Sofia, Gus, & Luzy, Diane & Cassie; & with more thanks to Pam, Leandro, David R, David D, Rodney, Wyn, Danny, Amy, Kelly, Eric & Holly for your ears and support; & to three old buddies lost—Mike Phillips, David Barber & my mother, Jean.

OTHER BOOKS BY SCOTT WITHIAM

Arson & Prophets (The Ashland Poetry Press, 2003).

Desperate Acts & Deliveries (Two Rivers Review, 2004).

TABLE OF CONTENTS

Can You Imagine This World?

There were all kinds of arguments and atrocities occurring on the earth's surface. There was one night's graceful smothering of snow. Then arguments muffled below the surface. Below one man's windowsill, buried along the buried lane, came, "Why bother?" And a response: "Why not?"—tulip bulbs arguing, their argument: whether or not to bloom. *Can you imagine this world?* he thought. He got them out of it by himself going outside, digging them up and throwing them into one paper bag. He drove them to the expansion bridge and stopped in the middle, got them out, lined them up one by one on a steel girder, precariously leaned them against those big bolt heads and said it: "You're bulbs, not bolt heads." "What's going on?" one asked. He snapped their picture, then said, "Bulbs without a flash." "What is this?" another more officiously demanded. "Look down," he said, "look at the islands." "There are no islands." "Yes there are," he said, "You just can't see them. They're beautiful, but under snow." A sharp blast of wind almost blew a few over. "Okay, okay," a couple of bulbs said; "What do you want?" a few more cried. "Look down," he said. "We did"; "There's nothing"; "It's bleak"; "It's frozen," were the answers. "Exactly," he said. "What's beneath all of this?" came the question. "Bingo," he said, "not a flowing but a flowering river." "We don't get it." "Neither do people," he said, "but you don't have to. Just come back home and do what you do." "And you, what will you do?" one bulb asked. They were on their way. There were flashing lights, a siren. "You were driving erratically," the officer said. "What's in the bag?" "What's it to you?" one bulb said. *"Please."* "Please,"

1

Scott Withiam

said another, "we want to get back. We want to get going."
"Are you talking to me, buddy?" the cop asked. "No," the
man said, "they are."

Two Rival Translations Explaining the Vanished Valley Dwellers

I.

In the early days the clouds came down to play,
pretended to be the mountains, mountains to walk straight
        through.
Rather than simply accept such a grand invitation,
the valley dwellers felt compelled to make
an example of it, like this: "One should not be anyone
other than who he or she is." The valley dwellers went inside,
locked their wooden doors behind them. Soon the whole
        valley filled
with muffled cries of "But who am I?" It didn't take long
for the clouds to move off, or for the mountains to come
        back clear
and edgy, leaving no way out.

II.

In the first days of indecision—where to settle?—the clouds
        came down
to be mountains. But none of the valley dwellers saw this
as an answer. They felt their best chances lay in making
        examples
of such events, and forged this living proclamation: "Never
        play
with where you are." That said, the clouds flew over the
        mountains

and on the other side dumped. Now it was clear. Now no
      clouds, just powerful
mountains close enough to touch, and close enough to hear
      the question
burning in each dwellers' mind: "But is this where I want to
      be?"
The mountains were insulted, and let loose upon the valley a
      mad river,
which never asks where it is, and takes whatever it's given.

Eternity

Two bow hunters were heading out of the woods after another day without bringing back a deer, when, at a puddle in a logging-road rut, tangled in some branches above it, dangling down, they spied one of those red-and-white fishing bobbers. "What the hell?" the first bow hunter said, but already angry and now concerned that they were losing light fast, kept on following the logging road out, grumbling, as he went, about any man fool enough to think he could catch fish in a puddle. The second hunter remained. *Although no hook is visible, the bobber surely caught us, caught our attention* was his first thought. And then, that the dangling bobber had kept time in an unoccupied way till now. Now it kept time in an occupying way.

Ovid as a Young Buck

Our park's forests are cool, lush, protected—maybe too much so? A young buck steps out of the woods and openly grazes in the meadow. Tourists grumble. They say park deer are too trusting. They want this guy to hide, be wild. Ovid's ears go up. *Hide wild? If so, no trust.* If only he could talk, not have to show. His skin shivers like the night stars still strung behind the bright sky—taut, ready to shoot off. "Right in broad daylight," says one tourist, "he's saying, 'You don't scare me anymore.'" *Scare?* Ovid's buck, half-facing away, has gone khaki. He's prepared for the conditions, dressed, so to speak, in a breathable shirt, two buttons undone at the top exposing the white patch of hair at his throat. That way he's the tourist, his thick neck strapped with high-powered binoculars looking more like a pendant. The buck half-facing us reveals tan haunches and a white rump. He's the bronzed lifeguard back at the motel pool—jumped in to rescue someone and his bathing suit slipped off. The drowning swam. The guard spared no one. The tail so busily switches.

The Leader

It got dark really fast while the seven small children gazed into their first campfire. "Man, right here, right now, *this* is heaven, *this* is what it's all about," said Dave, their burly leader. Half-nods only out of the kids. How would they know? What could they really see? As best as they could tell, the hot whole chicken legs Dave just dragged from the coals and placed at their feet were singed crisp black, the foil wrap melded to the skin. To the youngest child, the legs looked like little opened books whose covers dimly reflected the big fire. Each child had just begun his or her book. Dave fetched himself one and immediately broke its back. It gurgled. "Well, what are you waiting for?" Dave said. "This is as good as it gets." "Not done. Mine's not done," whimpered the youngest. Dave sighed, tipped his head skyward and under his breath mumbled, "There's always one." That's when a star fell, one with a long tail. The youngest sprang up, went crashing through the woods after it. Just as quickly, the remaining children followed. "Hey, what are you doing? Come back," Dave hollered. When it got too quiet, he stood up and looked around, puzzled at those glittering books. "Don't be silly," he yelled out, "they never make it all the way down here." "Come on," he yelled again, "we'll throw them back in." "Who?" went the youngest child. "Who?" the rest of the children joined in. "Who?" "Who?"

Food, Prizes, Tours, Plastic Surgery

Two stainless-steel tables spread with inviting home-baked sweets, operating. Resistance: brownies made hunch-backed by walnut halves breaking the surface, ugliness more inviting. But I had to sign up soon, if I wanted to ride the fire truck to no fire, or could, while waiting, just hold the hose at full force, which I did, planted my feet in the open field, braced myself and felt held down by the protective gear and helmet. But no professional from the office had time to chat about the weight I felt on my head from looking at everything going wrong with me. Or why real firemen sacrificed their bodies and put out real fires. Feet firmly planted there, I tipped over and the hose got away, did its own dangerous dance. I left that dance card to two surgeons helping out and went to where the cakes dripped with frostings a familiar color of cheap jewels and vinyl siding, where the cake wheel made of board and bright nails, when spun, whirred and wound down to a few ticks. And if the stiff ticker landed on the number written between two nails, the number that matched the number written in magic marker on the index card handed to me, well ... I could have died: I won.

It Would Take a While

Francis rose in the dark to walk a well-marked valley trail owned by the vacation inn. This was the first day of vacation and he wanted to set a tone, a pace for the two weeks ahead. He would venture outdoors as much as possible, immerse himself in the woods, in the lake, be attentive to the motions and sounds of wild animals, let the patterns of flora and fauna purge him. It would take a while. At dawn he showered, and still not in a vacation mode, routinely shaved. He stepped out of the steamy bathroom into the foggy bedroom, prepared for work. And then his wife unconsciously called from the vacation bed, itself a valley. "Shave," she said. "You're hurting me, my ... just shave, will you?" He woke her, to check in before checking out as the inn's brochure said to do. He mentioned her ultimatum given to someone other than him. "You're going to stand there," she said, "and tell me that you know better than me what I said or need?" He briefly stroked his smooth chin, and then ventured outside where the first light fell on the field opposite the inn and the chill breeze registered strongest on his naked cheeks. He got as far as the road, where he came to a purple-flowered bull thistle as tall as him. A few of the many loose milkweed seeds, dreamily floating in from a field, caught in its spurs. "What's it like," asked the thistle, "to have a clean face?"

The Immaculate Interior

My grandfather's days are easy now. He has lunch engagements, not to get out, not for the dining experience or exquisite food, like those crazy cooties (he means foodies); just to meet a guest. This way, it's not hard, when they meet, wherever, to get busy getting on each other's clouds. "Your mother," he says, "your mother is all wrong." It's not just a lot of huffing and puffing. According to him, what matters most ends up being close to that silly depiction of heaven—getting on our clouds, and therefore not *in* our clouds, where, just like in clouded family restaurants, a baby screams and the whole family, the whole place, really, gets lost in an endless search for one thing to make it happy. There's no proof, of course, and we think he's lost it, but he says that when they—he and his guest—leave the clouded family restaurant and begin to go their separate ways, outside they are always carried in the same direction— "What everyone in the family wants, isn't it—harmony?" he says—to the full parking lot across the street. Around them are clouds that neither he nor his guest noticed when they met. Among the clouds, they try to locate his guest's car, a silver Mercedes convertible coupe with the top down. "How can this be," he's been asked many times, "that there are always different people, but it's always the same fancy car?" "That's a question for your generation," is his answer. "I never tire," he says, "of its design." Always a clearing happens, and at that moment they find the car and whoever is with him falls to admission: "You know how some people say they're sun or water people or mountain people? Well, I'm a wind person. I've always loved the wind," the person says. And ogling the immaculate interior, stroking its surface, my grandfather says, "Isn't that something. I've always loved convertibles, how, after a very very very long ride, the wind still burns on my face, remains in my ears."

Boat Talk

Slips for sale. Under sail, sloops
heading out to sea. Boats—
anything loosely tied—discussed
at functions, at every meal out.
Over anything, boat talk. Dis-
gust. Over and out. Too far out.
New to town, my days on end
tipped trying to fit in only to be
fit to be tied; the more trying
to get shipshape, really
readied to ship out. Got
about as far as off-season
boats stacked in boatyards,
shrouded, shrink-wrapped,
white, very watertight.
About then I grabbed the wheel
and went "Man, if I'm not in
a boat or into boats, what am I?"
I sat in my car outside The Pier
restaurant with its pilings, waiting
and waiting for my daughter
to be dropped off from her school,
home of the Vikings. The Vikings!
Stroke, stroke, stroke your boat.
Relentless. One after another—boats
in the highway rotary
till an unfinished fiberglass hull hauled by
on a flatbed. *Un-christened, unfinished*

13

for now, I thought. I loved that. Did.
It was my boat come along—
fiberglass with give, room
for improvements, adjustments, settling.
Two red-eye-shift boat-factory workers
parked next to me.
The kid of the two wondered
where the hell that unfinished hull might go next.
"Never let yourself get that attached,"
said the old salt sitting next to him. "Dad,"
my daughter said, jumping in on the other side,
"Dad, where are you?"

Sweet Talking

A beautiful day, gorgeous
blueberries hitting and filling my tin pail.
At the same time, eating my fill. Some for now,
some for later ... 'two for tea / just me for you /
and you for me.' I don't know what happened.

Flush with a flush highbush blueberry bush,
I said, "I had a father. He's dead, but when living
in Florida he grew something too—tiny oranges.
The natives called them bitch oranges.
No need to pick them, but he did,

brought them inside, lined them up
on a windowsill, so he could look out
and say, 'No amount of sugar turns
these sour bitches around.'" "Uh,
we're no longer talking fruit here, are we?"

said the bush, and as it did, some branches parted
near its center. "How many women left him
or did he leave behind?" the bush asked.
Hidden inside the bush was an empty bird's nest.
I took the largest blueberry from my pail

and dropped it in. "For every egg
my father ever laid," I said.
"That's it? One blueberry?" the bush said.
"You expect that to fly?" "Yes I do," I said.

"You're that sweet." "Father," the bush said,

and all its leaves raised shiny-side up, "do they
ever learn?" "Your father's still alive?" I asked.
"What does he do?" As the bush shrank,
a bird broke from the nest.
"Makes himself feel
good," the bush said.

Twelfth-Century Church Carved Inside a Mountain,

chiseled out of stone. Such cold
rooms such human drive—
to physically make another world
available. The metaphysical.

This anteroom full of coughing tourists—
what drives us? Association: Oh, Howe Caverns,
oh tourist trap, stone teeth and bowels
backlit like an Italian restaurant.
I traveled three thousand miles
only to see you. Oh, other-
worldliness—
the places I've already been. Oh,
man standing next to me
registering disgust with the tombs,
the bodies one had to walk over
in order to get to worship.
Oh, me.

Delays, Psychiatric Hospital Administration Building Groundbreaking

> *The one who comes is not one of mine, an ...*
> *I see, but I do not ...*
> *I see, but ...*
> *I see ...*
> —*Gilgamesh,* Tablet X, Column iv

The governor of ... late ...
... days and days of rain, it held for him ...
but the wind came up. And ...
The small school band scheduled to play
sat and ...
and ...

Dressed in his marching best, all black
with gold piping, epaulets and ascot, the band director
tossed two clothespins into each musician's lap, he ...
"All you're getting. Don't lose 'em, boys and girls.
Use 'em. You don't want to be lost, not today."
"Get lost," one patient shouted. "This is all you get." And
          then ...
... flew ... swarmed, all white ... silenced.

... when the true governor arrived.
"This is it," said the director...
the band's instruments in unison played. But the wind ...
whole sections of the fanfare ...
landed late, off. Like this ...

18

Then the patients ...

"Pick it up," said the director.
Patients held their heads because the governor held his ...
Silver hair in place, signature trench coat flapping, he ...
... to the podium.
"Oh, that's what they do!" another patient squealed,
hoisting up a clothespin she found, still clipped to it
the first piece of sheet music that got away.

Loosed, unruly, flapping on a tripod behind the governor,
          the enlarged
architectural rendering, the finished ...
... men holding up a picture.
"How many does it take?" she ... , the same one who ...
Ignoring ... rapping his knuckles on the podium, the
          governor ...
"This is what you've entrusted me to do. I ... and ... will ...
promise ..." The wind gusted.
Sheet music spread over the excavated lot.
"... new construction, new hope."

Prophecy's Tool

Wandering behind the new house,
picked up that kids' short cut,
which cut just short of some undeveloped house lots,
and somewhere back there he kicked up
and picked up the not-so-ancient whiskey bottle,
stayed on trail till spilled
into an older neighborhood, onto a ball field
next to new, plain-lined church. There he caught the bottle
in what was not out of bounds, did a little end-zone dance,
shook it. Some metal flecks from the remnants of a screw
       top
faintly sounded inside. The bottle reflected
one of the iodine windows of the new church. Inside that
       church,
glowing, red votive candles huddled. Upon what were they
       reflecting?
Periphery, he thought, head-on, the walls of stimuli,
but a glimpse of something greater in the margins,
prophecy's tool buried, except when exercised
in the church of contact sports
watched by fans off in the margins; exercised
only by athletes on the playing field
so to help them see an adversary's approach.
He was sure of this. He was good at this.
He held the bottle up, shook it again, tipped it skyward,
peered into it for what happened next.
Across the street, a guy the size of a lineman burst
upon his porch. "Doin' that right here?" he said. "Dude,

really. What don't you get? Take that someplace else
before I have to come down there and do it for you." *Y
ou have no idea what I'm doing,* he wanted to say,
but yes, the big guy had his own idea of that.
But it's not what you think, he wanted to say, but
yes, it was as much what the big guy thought. *Someplace else,*
he thought, and looked into the bottle again. He didn't see it
       coming.
"Then why don't you," he said to the big guy,
already on the first step. "Go ahead,
come right down here and finish it for me."

Scott Withiam

In a City I Didn't Know

It was not an uncommon question to ask
a woman my age, with whom I was unacquainted.
In the midst of a boisterous summer dinner party,
both of us had wandered the host's backyard
to the same edge, an overgrown tangle
in which some children hid. I thought of mine.
"Do you have any?" I asked, and then had to watch

any light inside of her dim. In a city I didn't know—
and hoped I never did—her only child ran
in front of a school bus. I froze and watched how,
with one hand, she began to madly fan her face—
keeping down more than heat. With the other hand—
raised, open-palmed toward me—she conveyed
I know you didn't mean any harm. Then both hands rose

to the same position at eye level—those closed—
fingers spread, as if around a ball, of which she kept
in motion, as if to most accurately hurl, assailing,
and then finally did let sail. And moved not toward
but away from it, through a gap worn in the hedge,
which led to the street, which as she slid through it—
the hedge—more swallowed than filled in behind her.

Scott Withiam

Some Opera

Some backgrounds in Mary Cassatt's oil paintings—
the detailed patterns on walls, furniture and clothing—
dominate. Close up, attention drains. Off of the real subject

is the real subject. My mother-in-law has Cassatt's tastes—
the patterns, the finery in the background. Decoration,
so that everything holds together,

though it never does, moves in and out like spyglasses
in the hands of Cassatt's lady at the opera, ogling
somebody who must be somebody in the box,

caring nothing for what unfolds on stage
because it's better off. The phone rings,
my panicked mother-in-law tells me

a wren's trapped in her house. Can I come over,
get it out? Sure, I'll see what I can do,
though outcome isn't the matter. It's about loneliness.

It's always there when you look the other way. At least
once a week the VCR's on the fluke, the computer won't do
what she wants it to do, she can't open the bottle

of pills. Any excuse for human contact. Some opera.
The bird is only background, and it's not singing. "Here,"
she says, "put on these gloves." With the help of binoculars,

I've watched wrens sing. They give it everything they've got.
Like my mother-in-law, up close the bird's terrified, broken,

but do you think it really lets me grab hold? It reverberates
around the living room,
off those busy little print walls.

Door Out of the Underworld

I had in hand my stamped yellow ticket,
passed on information, a pencil-drawn map
on scrap, directions to follow to the farthest end

of the auto salvage yard for what I said I needed,
a door. Loosely, I had in mind a modern underworld,
the twisted, broken bodies organized

by make and name for convenience.
"Do you know what you're doing?" the gatekeeper asked.
"No," I said. "You'll learn," he said,

"it's easy." Right away I ran into a guy named Harry,
who squatted there, and sometimes hung around
during the day. He rummaged through

the front seat of a freshly rear-ended Skylark.
The underworld. From the front-seat side pocket,
he pulled an asthma inhaler.

In his other hand he dangled a miniature stuffed *49ers* blimp
meant for the rear-view mirror. Harry pushed the blimp
          through a fog
provided by the inhaler, and then went live:

"No, Jim, sorry, I can't see the field. I can't see a thing.
It's all clouded in. Let's hope it burns off soon
so those tuned in at home can enjoy the game."

It's just a junkyard, I kept telling myself. *Get in
and get out.* I did—with the '94 Toyota Corolla door.
It put my car back on the road. I kept telling myself that.

Watching Deer in a Snowstorm a Few Days after Oral Surgery, Recalling What the Dental Assistant Said

"*Why, this is the easiest part, dear, going under.*"
Envying the deer's grace, the ease
with which they recede. Never go so far
as to inquire about the afterlife.
"*Oh, in one percent of one percent of all the cases,
dear, patients go under and just keep on going and …*"
What really go on forever are struggles
on earth with speech. Or recovering from them. Yet briefly,
heaven is any deer's here in the dropped …
"*Just let go* … sparkling white … *That's it* … flakes floating …
        That's right,
dear …" Disappearing into snow. Whispering,
"*Can you still hear me?*"
Still breathing.

Sound

The deck party's host grabs and shakes your hand and quickly says his name, Dick King, as *dicking*. You're still politely smiling. "Don't you go there," he says. He peers down the bank toward the lake, squints, as if you did go there. You didn't, at first, but now *dicking* registers and you turn to look through the same dark woods toward the lake as Dick, just to politely hide your give-away face. "Put in a new dock in the spring," Dick tells you. "New," you say, but you're thinking about this formidable deck, known as June's deck—Dick's wife, June— for which the party has been created and pulled off, though no other guests are on June's deck when Dick is. And then you're thinking about the other new things Dick showed you: a Miata, a Ski-doo, a WaveRunner. You feel a little trapped till a man named Doc pops out, literally, walking into and pushing out the slider screen to rescue you without knowing. Soon Dick is talking to Doc on the deck about his new dock and Doc says he's got a new dick, where's June? And also that this party is such a good time, such a good idea. As good as any for one to pardon himself and go down and examine that dock, go down that steep bank in the dark, go tree by tree like a monkey swings tree to tree, only you're not swinging, just feeling your way along, till you do reach the dock and test it, jump on it and try to rock it back and forth like a monkey because Dick said of the dock, *sound,* also said of the sound "like fireflies frozen on, once you're down there," which you are. All the cottage lights are like fireflies, only then comes their frozen clatter to which you actually say, "porcelain, castanets," but that's the sound of Dick's June sashaying up with a plate full of Little Neck steamers. She proffers these on a paper plate, three plates, to be exact, left pressed together, so that the clams don't wet through. "June, Doc's here," Dick calls out, but June doesn't answer. For you, she wants you to know, she's personally poured into one condiment cup the broth for cleansing, and into another, hot butter, slicking to ease swallowing. "We've always been like family," June says, sidling up. "Really?" you say, looking at the gaping clams. "You look like Dick," June says, and without spilling, destroys the mosquito fat with blood sucked from her bare shoulder. "Who do you think you are?" June hisses.

Separate State

The family two docks down,
their chatter straining over the talk radio blaring,
in-laws, who never had kids, warning relative's kids,
"Too close, kids." Me on my dock thinking *No kids,*
so that's the reason the kids are too close,
but no breaks. The in-laws: "Stop it.
Stop horsing around." "Oh, go ahead,
fall in and hurt yourselves." *That,*
first thing Sunday morning,
first day of vacation,
along with their radio station's guest host's struggle to fill,
myself already having my fill
till over the radio, this desperate move
by the host: "Can someone name three states,
two divided by a river also naming the third state?"
My dock, the separate state I tried to fish
when the fat perch sized up my worm,
bobber, then me, slowly rolled,
its white belly signaling *Not interested*—
that perch taking me to that state
of a name I never knew,
nor his face ever complete; that teen
who never completely came out of the water, so to speak,
never bit on *here, the life,* as people say,
we live for, a dock, summer, family, fishing. That boy, too,
one day surfaced, rolled
through two business offices till pushed
to mine. "No need to explain," the boy said,

standing in my doorway, "I know you
really aren't the professional I need to see, I know
this really isn't the right place. Later,"
and bolted. "Listen folks," the radio host pleaded,
"I know someone out there knows the answer."
And so then, years later, mine: *Really isn't the right place*
later, remembering the stunned still, the state afterward
calling it a stir caused by the boy,
and its response a little thing
that shouldn't have upset anyone enough to jump in
that icy river. Shortly, two docks down
the guest host chirped, "Wait a minute, we've.............."
Splash—the radio kicked into the water,
so, for a few seconds, silence,
what, I thought, all our states needed, till one
child whimpered, "I didn't do it,"
and the father said, "No one did;"
and then: "Of course he did it,"
the sister-in-law said, "and now we'll never know
the answer. You're the father.
Do it. Remove him."

Sweet William

The book on gardens is inconclusive, maintains that a battle rages concerning the origin of the plant's name. Derived from William the Conqueror or Saint William of York; Prince William Augustus or the Duke of Cumberland? I have my own entry: The book is right on one count: *Sweet William* fills in quickly. One morning, a stranger's truck veers to the opposite shoulder, glances off a boulder, flips but lands right side up in a ravine. Following some other trajectory in time—a nice feature of plants, unless they spread too close to your house. I couldn't open the door. I couldn't get out. I was on my way to the abortion. I was first on the accident scene as the driver slid out bloody and stunned. There he lay. To be reminded, and then to see how many others drove right by, while I urgently waved for everyone to stop. Of all things, a laundry truck pulled over. Without hesitation, shrink-wrapped bundles of bleached towels, headed for a university, were spilled to cover him. Whatever's planted, give it a name! He shook from shock. I asked him his name. "Bill," he said. Not *William*, more highly regarded. "This isn't the first time this has happened," he blubbered. "Shh, shh," I said, "it doesn't matter. What matters is that you're still alive." I had to get going. I had to make that appointment.

Scott Withiam

On Reminiscing

I just found myself present
at our last beach trip
how many summers ago? Wading in,

we spotted a surf clam.
It had a creamy orange tongue
twice as long as its shell,

which helped it launch
into the sweep of a passing wave.
As I am doing. And don't clams

feeding filter every grain
from wherever they land?
I cherish life so much

that I wish to live it all
again. But wasn't the far-off
just as bright and beautiful

even though we missed it,
our heads elsewhere?
"One hell of a way to travel,"

you said, as the clam vanished.
We tried to follow it,
till someone else called us
in. As happens. As it will.

Scott Withiam

Off Base

Fuel, long ago, that car filled to the rear window
with newspapers and monthly magazines,
those mixed with white envelopes,
all loosely cascading over the front seat,

pooling on the floor around the feet
of the woman driving it, the woman we called
the woman with the car full of newspapers,
always coming out of nowhere, but once sighted

by us kids hanging on the street, called,
"*Emergency landing!*" For loaded down
as she was, she tipped a wing too far, rolled,
spilled, caused an explosion, because as it was,

when she pulled over, she dug out,
popped the sprung door—*boom*—pushed back
leaking papers, in front of the post office brushed off,
straightened on her way in to see Stewart,

the postal clerk. Stewart, called *Stump.*
Not as a result of explosions,
more because he stood there and cut to the obvious,
like "B-52's up there refueling again,"

though never a word to the woman
with the car full of newspapers,

just the exchange. For her,
an unclaimed magazine or newspaper,

an occasional dead letter that Stump saved,
that Stump told us, once we were ready to take it,
was the least anyone deserved, a place,
even if it wasn't real. Fuel now,

the sound barriers breaking—the usual,
living off base—or to see, then, a B-52 refueling
in flight, to pinpoint, high overhead,
two shiny bodies connected by what looked like
a plastic straw in a milk carton.

Scott Withiam

On the Way to the Casinos

"We're not junkies or killers or something.
We're just going gambling for one day.
Can't you just shut up and enjoy it for what
it is?" That was John. He drove. "Maybe
we're not directly responsible," I said, "but by ..."
And that was Jeff, who, bouncing around in back,
reached around the headrest, clamped
both hands over my mouth. And that's us,
just like that coming to a stop at a major intersection,
which, years before had no stoplight, just crossroads
that everyone shot through without looking.
So wasn't gambling human nature? And beyond fun
and the question of real jobs,
didn't gambling provide false hope
or an old jolt of risk in order to feel alive
when we felt dead and helpless? What
was wrong with me? Gambling was religion.
Nothing was wrong with me, if something better
was coming. If it made me believe,
then at that same intersection where we sat,
not too long before, a boy sat there in a car
with his father. A fight spilled out of the bar
before breakfast. Two drunk former farmers.
"That," his father said, "is their job now,"
and the father's job, though a salesman,
was to sit tight till the cops arrived,
but as soon as they arrived
they let the farmers keep going, beat and beat—

because we're entertainment.
I wasn't that smart. No, I wasn't.
But then the light changed,
and John, Jeff, and I continued
till it was like the casinos, so quickly upon us,
sprung out of those fallow fields.
And Jeff's hands—tapping the seat behind my head—
jumped to roll down a window,
so he could hang half himself out
and fist-pump *ka-ching, ka-ching, ka-ching*
in the air. And John howled, "Ka-Jesus,
just get me there." And able to shout, I shouted,
"Blow the horn. Blow it." And even reached across
to hold down the horn all the way in,
because I believed. Or more, now I believe
I saw the bloody farmers—
distracted by the horn and our showing—stop,
their arms come down, their look
at each other, as if *What are we doing?*
And then we're there.

Summary

... there is a story given, differing from the rest .... That the women of the island [Cyprus] received Ariadne very kindly, and did all they could to console and alleviate her distress at being left behind. That they counterfeited kind letters, and delivered them to her, as sent from Theseus, and, when she fell in labor, were diligent in performing to her every needful service; but that she died before she could be delivered, and was honorably interred.
—Plutarch

Plutarch, I love you, but your under-dressed summaries smell suspicious. This one, when returning to the text, rereading, broke out "women of the island" as *women of privilege*. There was a need to dress. "Received Ariadne very kindly, and did all they could" slipped into *provided her with separate quarters and three slave girls still suffering the loss of husbands defending their homeland against Cypriot invasion, during which each girl's infant had been ripped from her arms, quieted then placed in a Cypriot home, homes of the women of the island, and on that island the slaves' children promised safe lives only if the slaves faithfully served and kept quiet about the past.* "Who else, who better suited," said a woman of the island, "to attend longing?" Talk about summary! I felt the slaves drag to Ariadne, clench, silently attend to "her distress at being left behind." But when carrying the child became difficult or mental burden worsened—hard to tell which—I heard *"Find those inept girls something else to do. For gods' sake, we'll take care of Ariadne on our own."* I watched, Plutarch, the women of the island write and the slaves deliver your "kind letters," sit with Ariadne, listen to her read aloud. The girls knew the words to be counterfeit, but considering the survival of their own children, held the facts inside. Each letter placed Theseus on an unknown island not unlike one the slave girls saw when wishing to be with their murdered husbands or to escape with their children. He was coming. That Theseus repaired his ship, grew nearer and nearer to departure only fueled Ariadne's desire to hold the baby in and for the slaves to throw every "needful" ounce into its delivery, Plutarch. The father should see his child.

Roof Too Small

The sun popped out and some children at the outdoor mall's playground ducked into some blue plastic tubing and began shrieking—for what reason, who knew—so that I couldn't hear the man who had just sat down next to me. His mouth moved, but no sound came out until I heard "… well, I do!" *Understood the children?* "It's Bobby, by the way," he said, "not Bob. Jesus, those kids." "Bobby," I said, "I don't think I know you." "Sure you do," he said. "Broke that high-school rushing record." Bobby gave a wink to the kids' babysitter sprawled on a bench. "Broke a few hearts too." The reclined sitter was too busy staying awake, struggling between holding open and following a thick novel or letting it fall to make a roof too small over her. There had been almost too much sun for an early northern spring. Bobby's face, though, was pale and rimmed by his bomber-parka hood's fake fur and yet he said that he had just spent the best winter ever in Florida, where he sold a line of scented tanning lotions under the name of Golden Glow—also known as *GG* on the beaches—and had at least eight lathered ladies on a chain on any given day.

How many centuries before, under the same northern sun, had Horace run into that old acquaintance at the Coliseum, who had ventured home for good from a faltering, far-reaching colony, but right away bragged about going back to that good life, the number of slaves he held, the way men in public places had always done—lied, embellished? *Now,* I thought, *I know Bobby.* The same sun. You couldn't hide from it. To Horace's joy, the only woman in Horace's entourage exposed the braggart, and soon Bobby unzipped his hood down the center and shot the sitter what was left of his killer smile, and *here we go again,* I thought, but no; by then the sitter was sound asleep, safe beneath that book. So then, here was my story—a sun so hot that there was no possibility of altering the way men for years kept behaving badly, but this once one man spared full exposure. No, not that either. Bobby grumbled "Who needs you?" Never mind the sun; he wasn't even talking to the sitter or the children, but to the tatter of white towel tightly held inside his fist, now spread across the palm of his open hand. The tatter had once been a whole gym towel, he said. The year he broke the rushing record, it had marked a hidden spot he and his sweetheart went to, and after loving they wiped with it and hung it back in the sumac, where it flapped at the tourists flying through till the next time. "But never again," Bobby shouted, "this is the last of it," spinning it propeller-like as he left, then flinging it, though it didn't go very far. There were tatters all over the playground. When the sitter woke to go to one of the crying children, without thinking she picked one up to keep her place in the book where she left off.

Of the Future

A yard overrun with rabbits lazily hopping in the dusk, as it always has been, here and there stopping to chew. Holes everywhere. One would be wise to stop there, when it comes to a view of the future, but I've never been one to stop. This morning, I took a walk. I happened upon a rabbit tail. Whatever being in pursuit of the rabbit came up short, got just the tail, spit it out; or consumed everything but the end. Futures make me jumpy. Here I am hopping around the yard. And there are my kids perched at the window snacking, watching me. The backlight of their TV and its shifting images place them in a lightning storm. *Lightning, a row of little Frankensteins, ghostly figures needing to be charged*—that image has gone to bed with me more than once. I don't remember my dreams, but I sometimes drive to the thrift store for no other reason than to look at the remains of lives attempted and given up or gone, just to fill them in again. This afternoon, I was confronted there by a beautiful woman—always a beautiful woman at the thrift store. This one wore a vintage flower dress that I began to nibble. Why am I always nibbling? "I know what's on your mind," she said. Did she? She was trying to work a hair inside her mouth to the front of her lips so to remove it. What did she have to do with that tail I found earlier in the morning, the future? She said that she had been like a show on TV— only what happened *to* someone else. "I'm taking charge. It's over," she said. "I just bought another house, came here so as to furnish it with items used by other people so I'll never have to live there." I left a huge hole in her dress.

Garish

Scent of hibiscus. The overpowering
perfume of our maid. The skirt of the foyer light

she stood under placing her
in a 5th Avenue display. The length and curving back of her

pink nails—petals of a jungle flower.
The tips of those petals peeling back

the blanket swaddling our adopted daughter
like a flower

inspecting a seed in its pod,
if that were possible. The baby powder rubbed all over our
      baby's face,

worked in; the maid saying, "Oh, oh, so dark. Soooo dark,"
all the while stroking between thumb and index finger—

deftly, no nails touching—the flesh of our baby's broad nose.
The assured look on the maid's face, which said *Anyone can*
      do it;

begin now and you may stretch, thin, straighten it out. One
      after the other
she drew our weary hands close and showed us the way.

Never mind that we had been lost in that winding city
built by conquerors. Never mind the dark

16C church for a moment sealing off the chaos and
        confusion
outside. Never mind the diffused light of the dome

like a flower head drawing us toward it,
and once under it, how our eyes strained

into it. Never mind
that we had argued over which one of us had said it, Garish,

the stiff arms of Christs bursting through
sparkling walls. Like heroes. Or thieves

who could not be stopped.
It didn't matter who.

We're Not Making Love Tonight,

my love said. A truckload of rotten cantaloupes
dumped in a vacant lot behind the warehouses.
All that work and energy

to get it to a mass of featureless heads
sinking into one moldy mess. Who isn't tempted
to say *waste* and let them go all the way,

keep walking? My neighbor: Sally.
Sally, as she always does, pulled something out of it:
a melon crate; wrenched it from that pile abuzz with bees.

Un-stung, she took it home dripping, hosed it down,
let it dry in the sun. Bone dry, she covered it
with *Blue Night* velour,

which, she said, always wants to be left
lustrous. "Leave it this way," she said,
stroking it, but I wasn't sure on which stroke—

forward or backward—she left it.
I needed to find out.
The velour she found years ago,

washed and put away until it spoke.
That was the day after the dump.
It said to her, "This is the moment

I've been waiting for! Now I belong wrapped around the ribs
of that crate to make a nightstand."
That's how Sally talks, like "Pulled over

and pulled tight around the crate
then nailed down, the crate won't wiggle.
Even stood on end, won't wobble."

Nor will her reading lamp,
placed upon the nightstand, move,
I thought, when I heard that.

She's reading in bed undisturbed
and at least the story she wants to read
isn't interrupted. But not that night.

It was hot and the wind blew. Her window
went wide open and her lights went off, and I heard
Sally say, "You shouldn't be left flapping like that.

I'm putting you in a better place."
She talked to a book.

Of Your Poem

How you use the *I* to step away and go on and on about yourself without offering much but language, distance, and futility is way too close to the way I feel when talking on the phone all day to people losing their homes to banks, who ask, "Should I just walk away, start all over again?" "Yes, go ahead," I today said to a caller, while thinking of your poem, and then I really took off: "Go ahead, just float as you already are, without a real or final answer, like a haunted spirit. Yes, if your house is, then all our houses are haunted. "Don't walk away, run." Click. My mind ran to *Night of the Living Dead* or *The Dawn of.* When listening, reading, or watching, as I'd done, as I was doing, it was the victims which worried me most. They deep-down knew the answers to the tragedy forming before them, but looked for someone else for an answer. They trusted no one they knew or saw, but wanted to trust anybody and everything they couldn't see to offer a solution. The former job of poetry! The company I work for now a business of it. I know, you merely asked what I think of your poem. These were not the intended results. That's what listeners are hoping for.

The Smallest Know

Under the sign that said *PRODUCE*,
three lifetime clerks in long white coats
quietly stacked pears, till one clerk said,
"I've noticed the shape of hourglasses
in the relief of the packed pears."
And a second clerk chimed, "Time relieves nothing."
"Initially, even a bruise can be succulent,"
said the third clerk, and sighed.
Out of them all, one pear spoke:
"But don't let anything stand for very long."
"Sit. Stop it! Get back where you belong,
you little shit!" screamed a mother to her son,
who had unbuckled himself from his shopping cart
shaped like a fire truck. "Man, there's our future!"
said the first clerk. There was a hissing sound—
the green produce being misted from overhead.
"The child thinks that heaven is crying,"
said the second clerk. "The smallest know," the pear said.
"Then what would you suggest?" asked the third clerk.
"Get busy," said the manager, as he approached.
"As usual," said the first clerk, "he's going to
give that boy a piece of fruit to shut him up."
"Hand him the talking pear," said the second.
"Shine it," said the third, "shine it.

Scott Withiam

Hey Now

Like none of the mall's chains are open yet.
Chains, and not too far away
my daughter takes a college entrance exam to gain,
in short, acceptance, in the long run, freedom. En-trance.

Wandering into a mall with nothing to do.
I hope her mind isn't so much stuff
inside without anything going on.
'Every sha la la la, every whoa oh whoa oh'

goes the piped-in Carpenters' song. O Karen,
I too have had failed obsessions with living
by consuming nothing. Christ, here they come—
a klatch of early-morning power walkers to

'Hey now, hey now, don't dream in slo-mo … Don't
dreammm …' is right. No one does.
No one has to. Everywhere, the corporate outlay.
Then trends to use up presently unused, otherwise-occupied
            prime space.

Like these early-morning off-hour power walkers.
Going nowhere. And exercising someone else's idea. Hey
now, *that's* getting accepted? My poor daughter. *Squeak*
go the power walkers' sneakers. Squeak, squeak,

squeak. Come out like little rats. Squeak. Hug the wall.

State-of-the-Art

Smack in the middle of a state-of-the-art cruise ship was built an oblong, reinforced, metal-lidded latch. Under the lid was a shallow pool in which a crocodile floated. A few wires attached behind the croc's eyes tapped the reptile's ability to be, more than look like, a log. That's what kept the ship stable on any state of sea, while every imaginable form of entertainment occurred without a hitch. Since confidence in the ship's advertised modern righting system was crucial for the guests' sense of safety and assured entertainment schedule, and subsequently, large sums of money for ownership, dependence on crocodile *logness* was kept top secret. As if to compensate for this secret or to believe it could be kept, ownership demanded 24-7 maintenance and cleanliness aboard the ship. One young woman on the deck maintenance crew was a promising artist exiled from her own destabilized country. Her job was to keep the area around the righting system clean. She wore knee pads and thick rubber gloves and scrubbed on her knees during the lonely graveyard shift. One early morning, the ship snug in harbor, all guests sound asleep after a full day of shopping in port followed by tropical buffets and lively island entertainment, the exile opened the tank, disconnected the righting system and let the croc out of the pool. He stood. She shook off her rubber gloves and helped him out. She handed him a cigar kept for distinguished guests and lit it. They circled the quiet main deck together, listening to only the sounds of the sea beyond the harbor and his tail dragging on the deck. On the second loop, she removed her knee pads. He let the cigar smoke seep out the long rows of teeth on either side, did not blow smoke out the two holes of his snout. Noticing the two wires trailing down his back, she commented that it appeared as if he had his wires crossed, a Western turn of phrase that she had recently learned, which, given her unstable past, and her new life working on a cruise ship, made absolute sense to her. The croc responded by saying that, no, his wires couldn't be crossed; he was, however, unattached for the time being. At this moment, she untraditionally asked him to wed, and then slipped a knee pad over each of his stubby arms as one might a ring. He flailed like a panicked child, one who wore water wings. This image brought her delight she had not experienced for years. Soon a very sleek boat pulled alongside the ship and the two were separated without incident. The exile was removed from the ship and the croc dragged back to his tank and hooked up. All staff was told that she was fired for failing to clean. No mention was made of there being a threat to the ship's safety or the fact that the exile easily unlocked the heavily secured tank and then had the crocodile move in amazing ways. No one asked how or why.

Landscape and Interiors

A lot bulldozed.
Hooked to chain-link loosely thrown up, the sign
that said *Build to Suit* with the *Will* torn from it, balled up
and blown away. I wanted to stick, for just a minute, to what
I believed once existed: a German restaurant,
the beer good and cold, no matter what unfolded—beer,
and dirty, stretched foreign flags nailed to the tongue-
and-groove knotty pine walls, walls tacky
to the touch, though of a darker amber, and thicker
than that of the flypaper

dangling like a chromosomal helix in the kitchen.
Not one fly on it. But in our genes? There were the authentic
          dusty steins
from which no one ever drank
billed as the *Largest Collection in All America,*
which now no one could ever dispute. Gone,
the bar's many disputes over nothing
of consequence. Now just nothing of consequence, a lot,
a lot of time to go on and on
about steins stacked below the bar, lining the shelves high
          above it,
and also above the booths, hugging around every corner.
Finally, a subject upon which comfort could be
found. Who didn't adore a booth? Who had not gone
far out of their way before just to sit in one?
And stopped. What was it about booths?
It was the instant invitation to slip in

sideways rather than land directly on
anything. It felt safer.
Then why was I sitting in an imaginary booth in an empty
        lot?
It was the best time ever
to talk
vision. In a booth one down from mine
sat another man looking right at me.
A stein had just fallen on his head. Fact. I saw it.
Opinion: "Of course,
that's the reason that the restaurant went under!" Opinion:
"Not true. How many German restaurants have you seen
that made it along a beach strip?" I had to do something.
I left my imagination. I walked out, into the weeds
and four-foot spikes of ailanthus on the other side of the
        fence.
I got out of my head
that man holding his head,
beyond the clunk and daze, his look
beyond embarrassment, to that of what hit him being of his
        own
making, his own fault. Otherwise, he would just sit
there to prove nothing had happened, when,
mostly, it didn't.

The World Struggles

And Bob has five ducks. He doesn't know how to distinguish their background or sex, and it doesn't matter because eggs get laid, and the ducks seem to take turns at everything, especially leadership, even if it is all about sex. Every morning a different one waddles them down to the nearby pond, where the water, okay, is not that good at all, but fresher than the water in the duck's little plastic blue kiddies pool, which Phil thinks Bob leaves standing too long. "Free and wild—the way it's supposed to be," Bob says. "Wild is convenient," his neighbor Phil says. "It means Bob takes no responsibility for his ducks, for their tearing up my yard." "Honk, honk," honk some Canadian geese watching from across the pond. *They're justifiably wary,* Bob thinks, looking out his window and thinking about that asshole Phil. *The geese don't want the life the ducks have,* Phil thinks, looking out his window and thinking about Wild Bob, that jerk. *Whose car is this?* Bob wonders, watching a strange car pull up to the pond and park. "He has a dog," Phil says, and leaps out of his chair. The stranger stretches into the trunk of his car and comes out with a brand-new tennis ball. *Brand-new,* Bob thinks. Phil too: *Brand-new.* The dog shivers in anticipation of release. The birds have already scattered.

On Happiness

Because Dave was neither stationary nor completed by marriage, family, job, community or nation, he became one of the wild geese warily nibbling in the field on the edge of his town, swallowing enough seeds, shoots, grains, and worms to take off, but by the time he finished it was night, time to rest, to join a flock, their cold night congress out in the middle of the lake, where the nature of happiness was openly discussed. What did Dave add when asked for his opinion? "Honk, if your child's an honor student." There was an immediate break in discussions. A few suspicious geese swam to Dave and crowded around him, politely nudged him to leave. "But I don't like to travel alone," Dave said. He was flown back home. At the edge of town, his escorts peeled off and returned to the lake discussions. On his approach there was at least contentment in daybreak as it spread a glow over the landscape. And contentment, too, in predictability: Edith Ward, who always shopped early for her three strapping sons, exited the grocery, although she carried much less than her usual load. And a little farther up the street stood Bob Boynton, long-time bank teller, his hands always so quick with large bills. Before beginning his bank hours, those hands fidgeted with his toupee in the front of one of the bank's barred windows. *Toupee?* Dave thought. *Bob doesn't wear any ... one small bag. Wait a minute, he and Edith?*—seeing each other, taking off for a picnic and more. As Bob opened the door to his sprawling white Lincoln Continental, for Edith, Edith saw Dave coming in low, coming right for the new lovers, his neck out straight and straining as if trying to get somewhere farther, which geese cannot help but do as they take off or land. "Duck," Edith screamed. Bob jumped into the car ahead of her, onto the floor, and covered his head as if a robbery were underway. "Get down, protect yourself," Bob ordered, till Edith reached inside the Lincoln, touched Bob's exposed noggin, and said, "I'm sorry, Sweetheart, I misspoke. I meant goose. We're safe. It's passed." They looked at each other, the positions they were in at that moment, and laughed.

Migraine

The king confined to his courtyard holds
his temples. On either side of him rise temples
riddled with bullets. Behind it all rise sheer cliffs
into which caves of riddles once easily dug—soft basalt.

Far below, the next assault: tourists buzzing
the once bustling square. Dead center, a tour guide leans
against the king's huge bronze head, points
through those pocked temples to the smooth cliffs,

bellows, "We used to see the caves as skulls
of the honored mystics who lived in them,
who once guided us. These days they're sockets,
the eyes plucked. They're filled with beggars.

No one sees...." A tourist straying off the cliff path,
craving, of all things, a souvenir, strolls
into a ravaged shop, door off its hinges,
any shelves still on the walls tipped clean, gingerly

steps to avoid the jars' jagged bottoms, staggers
only when his head glances off the rusty cage hung
dead center. The finch bangs back and forth.
The door is sprung open. Why doesn't it just fly away?

Scott Withiam

Pine Box Derby

after a letter from a Cub Scout Leader

Parents, Friends, Neighbors, Community,
Communities, I don't think that can be said enough.
Especially as a race in a race.
Everyone, more than we want to believe,
Has more
A minor part in the design of their vehicle
To race on the downhill
Track. We go By. The Ultimate
Rules: no engine but gravity. Agreed,
Staying on task, then, shouldn't be too hard.
One carves their own miniature vehicle out of an issued pine
Block. When finished, your son holds your life in his hands.
The idea on such an uneven playing field is for him to be
            the first
To let go, but more so, in that moment just before, poised
To accept that he does know his competitor very well,
That he is thousands of What-should-my-car-look-like?
            discussions at kitchen
Tables revealing everything is about wheeling,
About how close or far away the wheels are
Nailed to the axle. Nailed too tight
And you get skid. Nailed too loose
And there's chatter. If I may say so myself,
May the best man wins
Should be every man finds something in between
And all participation yields a badge.
And may your son too

Be on his way to another day far off
When he comes back to visit and speaks to us as an Eagle.

Scott Withiam

The Petty Snow

Winter's first snowflakes stuck together on their way down.
There were so many people upon which they fell who were not
sticking together. There was an unsnapped driving glove
fallen to the wet slop, looking like a tired tongue hanging out.
People awkwardly slipped away from each other, bodies taut.
Meanwhile, they looked up, higher up, for the highest
        mountain
hidden in a blizzard. It was almost religious. No one knew that
up there was an English-as-a-Second-Language teacher. Her
        car
had just spun out and ditched. She sat there. She could not see
the towns or people below, but considered how
the snow at higher altitude dumped in looser, world-torn
        tongues,
and thought how she had formerly thought how this
        horribly descended
upon the race. But here, she said, "Beautiful as it is, why do
        I try
to control my students' writings? Why, when life is, as one
        student
had written of heavy snow, 'like door after door shutting
        behind like,
real life getting more and more eearily quite?'" The teacher
        got out
of her car, stood in it, what her student called "the petty snow,"
and following one snowflake, the complexity possible in
        each structure,
each phoneme, each situation or moment, said from then on

what she would correct would be her pettiness,
so that there was prettiness. Could that make a big
        difference?
Remember the driving glove?
Attempting to drive over the mountain was that man
        wearing his other,
himself petty obsessed with a question: "What good is one?"
Not the deep question, What good is one flake or person?
but What good is one glove? Given the visibility,
he mostly saw his numb hand steering, till, perched on his
        naked hand,
superimposed like the sharp-eyed hawk hunched on a dead
        branch
and disappearing under snow, voilà: the teacher. He too
        stopped,
ditched, but could not see how she saw the snow
as a huge blank piece of paper, out of which now opened the
        only door
for miles, his door, and how suddenly—*suddenly,*
the word she warned her students never to use—a red, a rare
        hand
reached out—his hand—and helped her. Suddenly,
she jumped in, shook herself off, kissed and blew warm his
        cold hand.
And very unlike him, he made a claim: human feeling—
        maybe even love—
did not come back with pricks but arrived like talons,
        because his glove,

the one she had slipped off and now dangled between them,
what was that but some small beady-eyed screaming being
      carried off
to be eaten so that the bigger being could live? She
      wondered, she said, how long
before someone below found it, the other.

Slicker On

An orange Home Depot five-gallon bucket—
more than a few people depend on one
for what's encouraged. On its side,
going down in big white letters:
Let's DO This.

Let's. Inclusion,
there's a national bucket-load.
"Well, how are *we* doing?"
last night's wait person persisted,
but really she was pushing

for my order. "Look," I said, "*we're* fine,
but nationally, is there one side
you like best and might recommend?"
"They're all good," she said,
left and never returned.

Well, I liked this side: I walked out,
but *we* came along some anyway.
That's what I like about us, we come along
anyway. Even though the rain stopped,
our neighbor got out of *our* pickup

and put on *our* yellow slicker just so
our hands were free, so we could coax
our Home Depot bucket off the back

of our truck, leave it on our street and watch
our water slosh back and forth, back and forth,

while our black rubber hip-waders—
done wading, rolled down buccaneer-like—
swish-swashed against each other, against each other
all the way to our front door. Like pirates, we,
yet so unlike pirates we waded through our house,

turned on all of our lights
put on our favorite music, flopped
into our bed and fell into our sleep. *La différence?*
We slept with our slicker on.
Our yellow slicker under the lights left on

retained the persistent sheen of smelt
in the orange bucket—"Three or four human races,"
the neighbor said last night, "not much
to bring home," which I just now included—
three to four smelt caught upstream mating,

slick in their own slurry, abandoned.
Sperm and eggs
because in the beginning beings want
to continue, and then: *they.* But we
couldn't forget that

this morning the rain came back,
and unlike those smelt we slipped
out of our back door without
changing. Hood up, slicker on,
we couldn't have come out any better prepared

for the day. And we held our head
high, as if we planned it that way.

Scott Withiam

Pastoral

O to stretch out in a meadow with a few friends, be approached by goats without names—not Marble Weight or Billy Sue, but goats 606, 608, 722. To move off, break into song: *They givin' you a number and take away your name.* For Ed McMahon to come up in a different field, because that's who does. And Johnny … Johnny Weismuller, because the man who sang the secret agent song, his name's Johnny what? Rivers. But really only babbling brooks. O anyway, Weismuller, because he's the one who could really swim anywhere. And Lo, to wrestle fake alligators in those breeches. Lo, the gulf swing of these, my breaches, not a soul hurt or killed. Gerald Ford. Saying what? That it's the numbered average days that bonk, that made me roam as far as I did; meanwhile, under the clouds of a bald day, missing the friends I loved and who loved me? No way! O to return and among loving friends announce, "Let's mark well our days together, and our goats too. Give them names like Weismuller and McMahon. Make them all count, as our children do right now by playing in the barn behind us." All so that one of us asks, "What do you think's going on up there? They've gone awfully quiet," so that everyone gets up and runs, runs together.

Don't Buck Love

Here comes the finch out of the mine.
They're alive! Well, almost. Out of the dark,
here comes the yellow school bus
full of sleepy, fragile lives,
for which we can do little
but bless the jostled heads
as they go on the same trip down
into the same town? Not this time.
This isn't just another day; love
is the much anticipated
field trip out, now and then, Baby,
and like the unexpected black-eyed buck
coming full head of steam, full rack,
full blast, two hundred pounds undressed
into the side of the bus.
'Can't you see the people just stop and stare?
Don't it make you wonder why?
I just happen to be a school boy sittin' there,
can't you see it in my eyes?'
I love you, because … "Stop it,"
you said, on your toes, there next to me,
face pushed to the window.
… *because I know how the body is*
like an accordion, which groans
when it's dropped. "I can't stop it."
"You're acting like a boy."
It's happened.
What can I do? Sure, bring in the experts,

Scott Withiam

their efforts to explain.
What can they say
to make us know, Baby, to show us
why a buck shows us what love is?
The mist off the snow
and what might come out of it,
the far orchard in winter,
a few apples still hanging on—
that's where it came from.
This is all anyone knows.
It got back on its feet in your eyes.

Lines borrowed from "What Can I Say?" by Boz Scags,
off the album *Silk Degrees.*

Memoir

quickly became popular, then corrupted,
although corruption was the case right from the start, but
    hell, it was always good
to know that, no matter what, one readily had access to
    some beginning,
something like My best friends and I were high school
    seniors ...
but if that was my case, none of my friends or I could afford
    cars. So we consumed,
instead, a lot of time with going nowhere
talk about the kind of car we would someday drive
or added in on a particular car racing through town that
    caught our eye.
Since I hailed from such an insignificant era, I found it
    necessary
to posit that the era, like its cars, was big, powerful, a Dodge,
a Dart with a gas-guzzling six pack, a Barracuda, a Cobra, a
    Sting Ray.
They came stock, but one still longed to customize. As I was
    saying of memoir,
one critic said that the biggest engine under its hood
might be the preservation of human innocence.
Dart, six pack, Barracuda, bite, sting—innocent?
But I could add a baby blue Mercury Comet with white interior
that appeared on the heels of the time of big fins,
so that a Comet could rely on the mere suggestion of tail.
The Comet was not sleek or fast, as the god Mercury
    connoted.

Nor was it muscle-jumpy like mercury spilled on a floor.
It traveled straight as a comet. As far as memoir, it was
        practical,
something, we'd say, our grandparents drove.
Only if we were desperate, we might take it, if it was handed
        down to us,
and do something with it. Probably jack up the rear
end. Memoir. I don't believe that it even matters
that we were seniors in high school,
except that senior label bears an attachment
to a taste for freedom, to a walk uptown to buy our own lunch
rather than stay in the cafeteria and eat what we were told
        was balanced,
and we exercised that freedom by walking into the air-
        conditioned Clover
Farm Market for one or two miniature pies—cherry or
        chocolate
or lemon with flattened meringue tails. That would be where
        a group of us
was heading when we saw that baby-blue Comet. It had
        wandered
(or was it steered?) into the oncoming lane and hit a rig
        head-on.
So little commotion. The Comet's hood was barely crimped;
        no radiator cloud rose
or water dripped into a pool. The truck driver's disbelief was
        our own.

He had come to a complete stop. They barely touched. How
    could they be dead?
That was the hardest part about memoir—it didn't look like
    it happened.
An old man's head was thrown back and his mouth was slack,
as if dozing in the surrounding muggy heat. Twisted toward
    him, his wife
looked to be doting, about to mention that he had missed
    some whiskers, there
was a patch of whiskers that he'd missed. That's all she wanted
to say, that's all she wanted, but we had to go back to school
where we went on forever, it seemed,
trying to come up with something better.

ACKNOWLEDGMENTS

The author wishes to thank the editors and staff of the following magazines in which these poems first appeared.

Alligator Juniper: "Some Opera"

AGNI: "Migraine; "Food, Prizes, Tours, Plastic Surgery"

Antioch Review: "Of Your Poem"

Ascent: "Of the Future"; "Summary"; "Off Base"; "The World Struggles"

Barrow Street: "Ovid as a Young Buck"

The Beloit Poetry Journal: "The Smallest Know"; "Hey Now"

Chattahoochee Review: "The Immaculate Interior"

Cimarron Review: "Roof Too Small"; "In a City I Didn't Know"; "Pine Box Derby"

Diagram: "Memoir"; "Separate State"

Drunken Boat: "Twelfth-Century Church Carved Inside Mountain"; "Sweet Talking"

e: The 2001 Emily Dickinson Award Anthology: "On Happiness"

5AM: "Delays, Psychiatric Hospital Administration Building Groundbreaking"

Fine Madness: "Boat Talk"

Green Mountains Review: "It Would Take a While"

Linebreak: "Don't Buck Love"

Madison Review: "State-of-the-Art"

Margie: "The Leader"

Ploughshares: "Door Out of the Underworld"; "Eternity"

Plume: "On the Way to the Casinos"; "We're Not Making Love Tonight"; "Slicker On"

Poetry East: "Two Rival Translations Explaining the Vanished Valley Dwellers"

Rattle: "Watching a Deer in a Snowstorm a Few Days after Oral Surgery, Recalling What the Dental Hygienist Said"; "Can You Imagine This World?"; "The Petty Snow"

Salamander: "Landscape and Interiors"

Sentences: "Pastoral"

Soundings East: "Garish"

The Literary Review: "Prophecy's Tool"; "Sweet William"

Western Humanities Review: "Sound"

SCOTT WITHIAM has been a recipient of the *Ploughshares* Cohen Award, and the *Two Rivers Review* Chapbook and *Drunken Boat* Pan-Literary prizes. His first book, *Arson & Prophets,* came out with Ashland Poetry Press. Recent poems have been published by *Agni, Antioch Review, Beloit Poetry Journal, Diagram, Ploughshares, Plume,* and elsewhere. He formerly taught college writing and presently works for a non-profit in the Boston area.